I0559570

A Beginner's Guide to

Loving & Healing Yourself, Everyone and the Planet Earth.

In praise of Gavin Muschamp's
1st version of this book called,
'The World According to 'Not-the-Guru' Gav'.

'A lively, playful take on self-improvement…'
(Kirkus Review).

'For anyone reluctant to venture into self-help waters…
Muschamp offers a safe, undemanding space to begin'.
(BlueInk Review).

In praise of 'A Beginner's Guide to Loving & Healing Yourself, Everyone and the Planet Earth'.

'This book is wonderful – it's warm and wise, it's funny and clearly written by someone with deep care for the planet itself and all those living on it.
Wish I'd found this book when I was in my teens, (or it had been given away in schools)'.

No-shoes-the-fish.   Amazon Review. *****

'It makes a poignant read that combines plenty of wisdom and insight, filled with practical tips and inspirational quotes you will want to re-read.
…a flawless, inspirational and helpful self-help and motivational guide with a unique touch. I have no choice but to award this brilliant book five stars'.

Aimee Ann.   Red Headed Book Lover. *****

'It's casual writing style…makes it an enjoyable read for those seeking meaning and purpose without the complexity often found in psychological or metaphysical discussions. The concepts are simple and easy to understand, making the book a joy to read.
I …highly recommend it to all readers'.

Luwi Nyakansaila for Readers' Favorite.

'…is more than a self-help book. It is a call…for individuals seeking to mend their relationship with themselves, their communities and the planet.
…a timely and vital read for anyone yearning to find purpose and connection in an increasingly chaotic world. This is a gem to have and to share'.

Elana Enger for The Book Commentary.

A Beginner's Guide to

Loving & Healing Yourself, Everyone and the Planet Earth.

Gavin Muschamp

Copyright © 2025 by Gavin Muschamp

Hardcover: 978-1-963050-96-7
Paperback: 978-1-963050-84-4
eBook: 978-1-963050-85-1
Library of Congress Control Number: 2024900280

All rights reserved. No part of this publication may be reproduced,
distributed, or transmitted in any form or by any electronic or mechanical
means, without the prior written permission of the publisher, except
in the case of brief quotations embodied in critical reviews and
certain other noncommercial uses permitted by copyright law.

This is a work of nonfiction.

Ordering Information:

Prime Seven Media
518 Landmann St.
Tomah City, WI 54660

Printed in the United States of America

**Front & Back cover –
Millennium Bridge leading to St Paul's Cathedral,
London, England.**

Home Page.

To everyone.
Let's create Heaven on Earth together.

Shangri-La was the original name of our house.
It refers to a 'mystical' heavenly place in the
Himalayas
and also perhaps to a blissful state of mind

Contents.

<u>Introduction.</u>

We are living in times of great change, individually and globally.

It can all seem very chaotic and frightening leaving us feeling depressed, angry and confused.

But it is also a great opportunity for us to really look at ourselves and to reconsider our lives.

It is an opportunity to move towards feeling more optimistic, peaceful and confident in ourselves and in our future.

To move from fear to love.

This book is a beginner's guide, helping you to get started.

And it could also be a useful reminder to those perhaps further along the path.

It is written in a simple way which is easy to read and remember. And there are also some practical exercises for you to work on.

I want to encourage you to think for yourself. Take self-responsibility and find your own answers amongst the pages here. What you feel drawn to and what resonates with your own 'highest' best self.

You might not agree with it all, you might not like everything, but I'm asking you to keep an 'open' mind. Perhaps some bits will speak to you and other bits won't. That's fine! Maybe some bits won't make any sense now but later they'll make perfect sense!

We're all going through big changes at the moment, whether we like it or not. So it's time now for us to look at ourselves and to realise that we can all do something to improve ourselves and our situation and to move forward together towards a better, wonderful world.

Gavin Muschamp.   Dec. 2023

Chapter 1.

In Search of Gurus and Masters.

For 1000's of years the only way to get 'spiritual' knowledge was to search out gurus and masters in remote parts of the world. Now that has changed. There are a lot more 'spiritual' teachers around today and the information is readily available in books and on the internet.

So maybe you thought I should look like this.....

But actually I look like this......   →

Chapter 2.
The old image of 'God'.

I used to think 'God' looked like
this, (approximately)….

An old man in the sky.

halo

stern look

white beard

pointed finger

white robes

book of judgement

(note –
probably not
wearing jeans….)

sandals

clouds

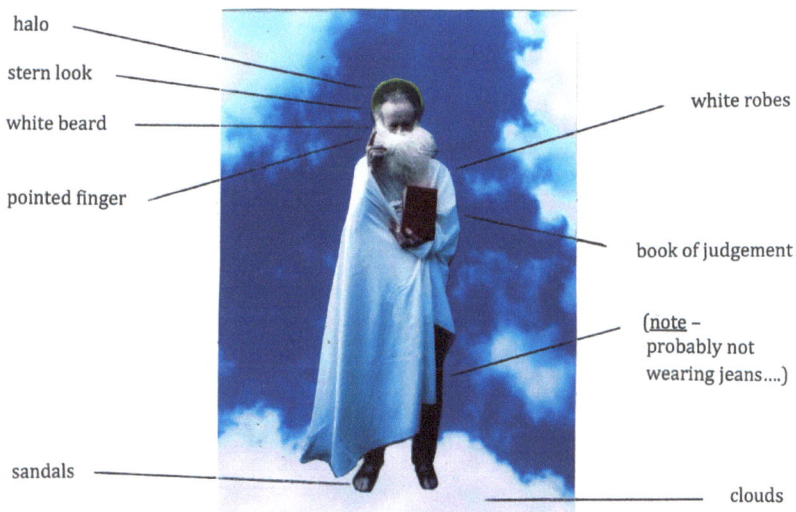

Note – this photo was taken on a Sunday.

But now I think this……. →

Be your own Super Hero,
(with God's help).

God wants us to express our own unique, 'best' individual self, part of him/her.

<u>Note</u> –
If you feel uncomfortable with the word 'God', feel free to substitute it for, Allah, Brahman, Jahweh, Akal Murat, Divine Being, the Universe, the Source, Spirit, Life Force, the Light, Unconditional Love, Higher Self etc or whatever feels right for you.

Chapter 3.
Love Yourself First.

'You yourself,
as much as anybody in the entire Universe,
deserves your love & affection'.
(Buddha).

3 – Love Yourself First.

- It's not being selfish!
  Come from your best 'Higher' Self.
  (Not the ego self which can be arrogant, conceited and with disregard for others).

- If you don't love yourself, you
  won't allow 'good' things to come to you.

- You can't love others either, until you love yourself.

- Be your authentic self.
  Express who you really are.

- Look after your whole self, physically, emotionally, mentally and spiritually.
  Remain in balance.

3 – Love Yourself First.
(Expanded chapter).

Many of us have been taught that it is selfish to love ourselves and that we must put others first.

But you can't give from an empty cup. You need to love yourself first.

Loving yourself can be difficult because we often judge ourselves and compare ourselves to others.

We might feel unworthy and not good enough or guilty and ashamed of something that we hide from others. (We might not want to appear odd or different and may have a fear of rejection).

But you can't hide from yourself.

The more you love & accept yourself, the easier your life will feel and you will start to feel more peace inside.

3 – Love Yourself First.
(Practical Exercises).

- Find a mirror and look yourself in the eyes.
Say, 'I love you' (to yourself).
This is not necessarily as easy as it sounds!
Be gentle with yourself.
You may want to do this regularly over a period of time.

- Some suggestions for loving your whole self, (physically, emotionally, mentally and spiritually)-
Exercise, walks in beautiful Nature, eat a healthy diet, eat organic, yoga, meditation, keep a journal, read inspirational books, do things you love and feel passionate about.

Chapter 4.
Find some quiet and stillness.

'Listen to the wind…..it talks.
Listen to the silence…..it speaks.
Listen to your heart…..it knows'.

(Native American proverb).

4 – Find some quiet and stillness.

- Amidst the busy world.

- Be in the present moment.

- Experience peace inside yourself & outside.

- Have some time on your own.

- Walks in Nature.

- Meditation.

- Listen to the quiet voice within,
  (intuition, Higher Self and God).

4 – Find some quiet and stillness.
(Expanded Chapter).

The modern world can be a very busy place where we are constantly rushing from one thing to the next.

And with Social Media there is a vast amount of information at our fingertips grabbing our attention.

But sometimes it's good to slow down and to relax. Forget those deadlines and all the things that need doing for a while. Find some peace.
Refresh yourself and recharge your batteries.

When you slow down you start to see things that you hadn't noticed before.
And it gives you time to really connect with yourself and others.

4 – Find some quiet and stillness.
(Practical Exercises).

- Try Meditation.
  There are many different types of meditation practice including, *Spiritual (often linked to spiritual & religious traditions, might include prayer) *Mindfulness (being fully present with your own awareness) *Movement (incl. yoga & walking meditation). *Focused (Concentration). *Visualisation (incl. guided meditation) and *Chanting (incl. mantras).
  So find what best suits you.
  You might want to try a local meditation or yoga group.

- Here is a simple breathing exercise.
  Put your hand on your stomach and take some slow, deep breaths. (The stomach moves out before the chest which enables you to take a deeper breath). Breathe in through the nose, (mouth closed) for a count of 4, hold for 2 and then breathe out through the mouth for 4. Repeat for a while. Don't strain.

- Go for a walk in beautiful Nature, (perhaps on your own so that you can more easily be quiet). Enjoy the peace and beauty.

Chapter 5

Earth is a place to learn and to have adventures.

'Nothing in life is so hard
that you can't make it easier
by the way you take it'.

(Ellen Glasgow).

5 – Earth is a place to learn and to have adventures.

- Possible problems, challenges, difficulties and 'suffering' come up for us all in our lives. They can affect every one of us.
  But it's not what happens to you, but how you react to what happens to you that matters.

- See problems as opportunities, (to learn, improve & grow). Suddenly they don't seem so bad!

- Think of life happening <u>for</u> you, not to you.

- Face your fears.

- Remember to enjoy yourself too!

5 – Earth is a place to learn and to have adventures. (Expanded chapter).

If you look back over your life so far, (and especially if you are older) you will see that everything happened for a reason. One thing led to another. (It might not be obvious at the time).

'So why did that difficult thing happen to me' you might be asking?
Although it can be very hard to take, we often learn the most when life is challenging. (If things are easy, we have learnt them already).
And as we grow we learn new things, we improve ourselves and we improve the world as well.
It can be very satisfying overcoming problems.

Also, if there is something that you need to learn, it will keep coming back to you until you do learn it!

5 – Earth is a place to learn and to have adventures. (Practical exercises).

- Try turning problems and challenges into opportunities.
  Rather than moaning and spending energy fighting problems, think 'What can I learn from this?' What is it enabling me to develop and what positive things can I get from this situation?
  Be gentle with yourself. It might be something you hadn't realised, (like a need to have 'boundaries' with some people).

- What are the main events of your life so far?
  (You might want to make a list).
  Good things and difficult things.
  What does that tell you about yourself?
  Are there any major stumbling blocks that keep occurring in your life and what can you learn from these?
  You can also see what you love to do.

Chapter 6.
<u>Embrace Change.</u>

'Change is never painful.
Only the resistance to change is painful'.
(Buddha).

6 – Embrace Change.

- Change happens – don't resist it!

- Life is constantly changing. It is impermanent and imperfect.

- If we can accept what is and be grateful and yet also work towards what we want, that can lead to happiness.

- Let go of the old, (what's no longer helpful to you) in order to let in the new.

<u>6 – Embrace Change.</u> (Expanded chapter).

The caterpillar will eventually change into a butterfly. It is inevitable, it can't be stopped!

Likewise in our lives, change is always happening, sometimes there is more change than at other times, but it is inevitable.

We tend to want to keep things the same because it can feel more comfortable and we feel safe with the 'known'.

Going into the new 'unknown' can feel scary, but once we embrace the change we often feel excited about experiencing the new and widening our knowledge and experience of the world.

<u>6 – Embrace Change.</u> (Practical exercises).

- What changes are you resisting? Make a list.

- Why are you resisting them?

- What do you want to keep and what do you want to let go of?

- Think of times in your life when change led to better things.

Chapter 7.
Be Positive.

'Smile and the world smiles back'.

7 – Be Positive.

- Be optimistic.

- Look on the bright side.

- Find ways to be happy.

- Smile!

- Use affirmations.

7 – Be Positive. (Expanded chapter).

We often have a choice of whether to be optimistic or pessimistic and whether to be happy or sad.
It's how you view what's happening to you and what you focus upon that determines how you feel.

Choose to look on the bright side as much as possible.

There will probably be some 'good' things and some 'bad' things happening in your life right now.

We can choose what to focus upon.
We can choose to focus on the positive.

The way to happiness is to be happy.

7 – Be Positive. (Practical Exercises).

- It is said that frowning uses a lot more muscles in your face than smiling! It can certainly cause more anxiety and stress to frown because that is an indicator of how you feel.
  So it's better, (and easier) to smile!

- Affirmations.
  e.g. 'I am happy, healthy, wealthy and wise'.
       'My life is full of love'.
       'It is safe for me to be myself'.

  The trick is to train your mind into new patterns.
  To start with it might feel fake saying, 'I am happy' when you feel sad, but the more you do it, picturing and feeling yourself happy, the easier it becomes.

- When you smile other people smile back, (or if you frown other people frown back).
  It is like a ripple effect.
  When you smile to others, they then smile to others, who smile to others and it goes on around the globe!

Chapter 8.
Gratitude.

'Happiness will never come to those
who fail to appreciate what they already have'.
(Buddha).

8 – Gratitude.

- We have so much in life already.

- Be thankful for the abundance you already have.

- Don't take things for granted.

- Say, 'thank you' for everything.
  Small & big things. Even difficult things have a purpose, (an opportunity for growth).

- Be generous – give as well as receive.

<u>8 – Gratitude.</u> (Expanded chapter).

It can be easy to find things to complain about and to look at what we haven't got.

But for most of us we actually have plenty already in many areas of our lives.

It could be family & friends who we can share things with. Or something simple that we often take for granted, like clean water to drink and enough food to eat.

It is also a wonderful feeling to give to others, (without any expectation of receiving in return). Seeing them happy is often reward enough.

It's good to have a balance of giving & receiving in our lives.

<u>8 – Gratitude.</u> (Practical exercises).

- Make a list of everything you are grateful for.
  This might include your family and friends, where you live, what you have already got, your talents and things you have already done.

- Say, ' thank you' often!

- Give something to someone else.
  This could be time & attention, help & support, care & love or a gift of something you know they like.

- Spread a little kindness around the world.

Chapter 9.
Manifest your own 'reality'.

'Reality is created by the mind.
We can change our reality by changing our mind'.
(Plato).

9 – Manifest your own reality.

- Follow your dreams.

- What you think about and focus upon is what you will get.

- Like attracts like.

- Imagine the highest good for yourself and everyone.

9 – Manifest your own reality.
(Expanded chapter).

We are all manifesting our own 'reality' whether we know it or not or whether we like it or not.
Because what you focus upon is what you will get.
If life is difficult that can be hard to accept. 'Why would I manifest this?' you might be saying.
But our thoughts are much more powerful than we realise.
And how we feel is also very important.
Like attracts like.
Happy thoughts and feelings will draw happiness to you.
But beware, unhappy thoughts and feelings will attract unhappiness to you.
So we can choose to change things for the better.
Difficulties often arise because of old thought patterns, (and sometimes because we are learning valuable lessons).

You are starring in the film of your life.
Hold onto your dreams, and if they really are yours, you will find a way to fulfil them.

When manifesting your 'reality', make sure it is not to the detriment of anyone else.
Imagine the best for everyone. There is room enough for all of us to achieve our dreams.

9 – Manifest your own reality.
(Practical exercises).

Basic rules for manifesting.

- Have a clear intention or goal.

- Picture regularly what you want. This could be in your mind or on a vision board, (put pictures, photos and words of what you want on a board and look at it often).

- Feel the joy and happiness of already having what you desire.

- Don't worry about the 'Hows'.

- The Universe will sort this out for you in the best possible way, (which might be in a way you hadn't thought of!)

  Note – if your desire is not actually the best for you, you might not get it, or if you do, you will soon realise that it wasn't the best choice!

Chapter 10.
Be Yourself.

'Be yourself.
Everyone else is taken.
(Oscar Wilde)'.

<u>10 – Be Yourself.</u>

- Take self-responsibility.

- Move from victim to self-empowerment.

- Don't just 'fit-in'. (Don't be afraid to stand out).

- Make up your own rules. (But don't harm others).

- Express your own unique, individual self.

- Find like-minded friends.

<u>10 – Be Yourself.</u> (Expanded chapter).

Find ways to be the real, authentic you.
Find some place where you don't have to cover-up and pretend anymore. Somewhere safe that you can let down your 'mask' for a while.

Dare to be you!

When other people can really see who you are, (and not just a façade you are putting up) you will start to make real like-minded friends.

This can feel scary at first because we tend to want to fit-in and be 'normal'. We fear rejection for being 'odd'.

But the truth is that we are all unique individuals.

The more you become and express your real self, the happier you will feel and you will begin to feel a great sense of freedom.

<u>10 – Be Yourself.</u> (Practical exercises).

- What is the real authentic you? (When you are not trying to fit-in and be 'normal').
  Sometimes we can forget who we really are.

- Make a list of your gifts, talents and interests and what <u>you</u> feel most passionate about in life.

- A good way to be yourself and find like-minded souls is to join clubs or groups of people with similar interests to you.
  You will immediately share some things in common without having to struggle to connect and without having to pretend so much.

Chapter 11.
Don't rely on others for your happiness.

'No one can give you wiser advice than yourself'.
(Marcus Tullius Cicero).

11 – Don't Rely on Others for Your Happiness.

- Don't try and please everyone else all the time.

- Don't worry too much about what others may think of you.

- Don't fight or try and change people.

- Tune-in to what makes you happy.

- You don't need a guru, (although sometimes that may help). Ultimately you have all your own answers within you.

- And remember, you can't help anyone else unless they want to be helped!
  You can't save the whole world on your own. Often people need to learn their own lessons and you may need to support them on their journey.

11 – Don't Rely on Others for Your Happiness. (Expanded chapter).

In the end no-one else can give you the amount of love and happiness you want.

You have to love yourself first.

If you are constantly trying to get happiness from others you will end up feeling disappointed, frustrated and angry.

Not even the most loving person in the world can give you enough love.

So stop grasping after love outside yourself.

When you start to find your own happiness within you, then you will automatically start to feel more peaceful and friendly, (and less demanding of others or yourself).

Then other people will start to feel less pressure and will start to feel more comfortable around you.

And you will start to naturally get the love and attention that you had craved, (without even trying!)

11 – Don't Rely on Others for Your Happiness. (Practical exercises).

- We are all unique, so what makes you happy won't necessarily be the same as your family and friends.

- Replace toxic people with supportive people.

- Try not to be emotionally dependent on others.
(So not relying on them for your happiness). You may end up feeling let down when they can't do this and they might feel it is too much of a burden to constantly try and make you happy.

- Instead get emotional support.
This means having someone to talk to when you are feeling down, but don't expect them to constantly help you.

- Take charge of your own life.
What makes you happy?
Find ways to get that without relying on others.
And you may also find other people who like what you like too.

Chapter 12.
Find your purpose.

'When you find your direction in life,
suddenly it takes off'.

12 – Find Your Purpose.

- Do what you love.

- Let your heart sing.

- Don't hide your light away.

- Let your light shine!

- Follow your heart to find your calling.

12 – Find Your Purpose. (Expanded chapter).

What do you love to do?

Follow your heart, your inner 'calling' or simply what you are most interested in.
(Not what you feel you ought to do to please your parents, friends or society).

It can be difficult to find yourself and to follow your dreams, (especially if no-one else is understanding or supporting of you). If you can find someone else, that's a great help!

But have the courage to be your 'real' self, despite what others may think. Find ways to be that in your life.

Inside yourself you will know what makes <u>your</u> heart sing.

So it's best to try and find a way to do that, even if it's not all the time.

Because you won't be truly happy until you fulfil your purpose.

12 – Find Your Purpose. (Practical Exercises).

- What do <u>you</u> feel most passionate about?
  What makes your heart sing?

- If there were no restrictions, (of time, money or family expectations) what would you do?

- Find ways to do what you love.
  You won't really feel happy until you do!

- Who do you admire and why?
  This could be famous celebrities and also other people you know. Include their characteristics and traits.

  This can give you a clue as to what you would like to be.
  (But remember that you are uniquely you!)

Chapter 13.
Use your full potential.

'It's never too late
to be what you might have been'.
(George Eliot).

13 – Use your full potential.

- Use all of your abilities, skills and passions.

- Get excited about life!
  (Don't get bored).

- Don't play small with your talent.

13 – Use your full potential.
(Expanded Chapter).

Focus on what you're best at, (as much as possible).

Sometimes it's tempting to play small with our talent.

We can become afraid of being so talented that other people will be jealous and won't like us.

But there will be other people who are super inspired by you.

They are just waiting for you to show your real self.

And when you use your full potential you will feel a glow of satisfaction inside yourself.

13 – Use your full potential.
(Practical Exercises).

- What are your best skills and interests?
  Focus on that.
  Make time for it.
  Make it a priority in your life.

- Make a list of all your abilities, skills, talents, gifts and interests. Find ways to use and express those.

- What excites you in life?
  Follow that!

  (Note – be aware of your limitations, your strengths and weaknesses. It's best to focus on your strengths but you will normally naturally know what they are because that is what you love to do).

Chapter 14.
You don't need to be 'successful'.

'Choose a job you love
and you will never have to work a day in your life'.
(Confucious).

14 – You don't need to be 'successful'.

- Money can't buy you happiness.

- 'Success' is expressing who you really are, (and not comparing yourself with others).

- Winning is not necessarily the best policy!
  (Helping each other is a win-win situation).

- Well done for not knowing everything!
  (Be curious and keep an open mind).

14 – You don't need to be 'successful'.
(Expanded chapter).

We tend to think of success as having a lot of money, possessions and fame.

But often it is an endless search that does not lead to lasting happiness.

Being successful is finding your own happiness by expressing your real self, whatever that is and not comparing yourself to others.

We all have our own 'special' talents, however significant or insignificant they may seem. We all have a unique place to fill.

It's a matter of finding the best way to be you.

And you might find your greatest happiness and success is in relatively 'small' and simple things like growing your own vegetables or giving your kids a fun time.

Whatever you enjoy most in life, that's where you'll find lasting joy and 'success'.

14 – You don't need to be 'successful'.
(Practical exercises).

- Where do you find your greatest happiness and success? (What do you enjoy doing and 'achieving' the most)?

- Make a list of all the things that you feel 'successful' about, (however big or small).

- You could also ask close family and friends what they think your successes are. (Maybe you hadn't realised some things which other people can see).

Chapter 15.
You don't have to be 'perfect'.

'Not being perfect is perfect'.

15 – You don't have to be 'perfect'.

- Don't try and please everyone else all the time, (it's impossible!)

- Accept yourself exactly as you are, (warts and all!)

- Doing your 'best' is good enough.

- Don't strive for perfection
  Go for excellence instead.

- Risk sometimes. Don't be afraid to get things 'wrong'.
  We often learn a lot from our mistakes.

- If life is a constant struggle you have got 'off-track'.
  See problems as opportunities.

15 – You don't have to be 'perfect'.
(Expanded chapter).

We often feel a pressure to be 'perfect' and to not get anything 'wrong'.

Do you sometimes think.....
'I should be doing better.'
'I should be achieving more.'
'I'm not as good or successful as someone else.'
'I am a failure.'
'I wish I felt happy all the time but sometimes I feel sad, angry or upset'.
'I'm letting everyone down'.

But by accepting and loving yourself exactly as you are it takes the pressure off yourself. Yes, aim to be your best self, but don't beat yourself up if you're not.

At the supermarket fruit & veg are usually only sold if they are 'perfect' in shape, size and colour. In society there is often an expectation that we humans should be perfect too, (in shape, size, colour and also in personality and achievements).
But we are all unique individuals. We all have our part to play.
Love those wonky carrots and mis-shaped apples.
And love your own uniqueness too!

15 – You don't have to be 'perfect'.
(Practical exercises).

- Do you feel that you have to be 'perfect'?

- Who is this pressure coming from? (Partner, family, friends, society)?
  And is it coming from yourself too?
  Make a list.

- Don't be too hard on yourself.
  And find ways to express your uniqueness and different parts of you in a supportive atmosphere.
  (Note - this might not always be with your partner)!

- When you try too hard and are afraid of getting things 'wrong', it can make you rigid in your thinking.
  Leave room for spontaneity and happy 'accidents'.

Chapter 16.
<u>Healing the shadowside.</u>

'Your whole self, (including the 'ugly' bits)
wants to be heard and loved'.

16 – Healing the Shadowside.

- Embrace your whole self.
  Bring your shadowside into the light of love.

- You don't have to be happy and 'positive' all the time, (although it's good to aim for that).

- Sometimes you need to embrace and acknowledge feeling sad, angry or depressed.
  But don't dwell on it.

- All the different sided of you want to be heard, loved and healed.

16 – Healing the Shadowside.
(Expanded chapter).

The shadowside doesn't necessarily mean evil.
It is the part of us that we are not wanting to look at.

This could be old 'wounds' from childhood and relationships or parts of us that we feel ashamed of or guilty about. We might not want other people to know about these things.

The more you try and push the shadow away however, the stronger it becomes.
Because it wants to be acknowledged, to be heard, to be accepted, loved and healed.

We don't want to wallow in the shadowside but we do need to acknowledge and accept it.

Then focus on the 'positive' and best side of ourselves.

Sometimes a forgotten or repressed part of us will turn out to be very 'positive'.
It might be just what we need to get back in touch with ourselves. And this might lead to a much more fulfilling and authentic life!

16 – Healing the Shadowside.
(Practical exercises).

- What parts of you are you hiding?
  Or are you feeling bad about?
  Make a list.
  Picture embracing and loving your whole self.
  (You could even imagine hugging yourself!)

- Some of these shadow parts of you might need extra attention and healing before you can move on in life.

- They may need some deeper expression in a safe space. Perhaps through art, writing, music or dance. This can be done on your own.

- But if this feels too frightening, finding other supportive like-minded people or groups can be helpful.

- Sometimes going to see a therapist or healer can be beneficial.

Chapter 17.
Gain knowledge, wisdom & experience.

'My destination is no longer a place,
rather a new way of seeing'.
(Marcel Proust).

17 – Gain knowledge, wisdom & experience.

- Be inspired. Be inspiring.

- Talk to exciting people!

- Learn from others.

- Better yourself and your understanding.

17 – Gain knowledge, wisdom & experience. (Expanded chapter).

When you increase your knowledge, wisdom and experience, you gain more 'awareness' of life.

You start to see things differently, often from a more expanded point of view.

That fresh perspective can open new doors in your life.

It can be exciting to learn things that you didn't know before.

And with that new understanding, you might become more accepting of others and yourself.

17 – Gain knowledge, wisdom & experience. (Practical exercises).

- What inspires you?

- Who inspires you and why?
  Make a list of all the people who inspire you.
  What qualities do they have that you would like to have? You may find that you already have these qualities but that you are not using them very much. You could focus more on these things.

- You might want to read inspirational books, go and hear an inspirational speaker or go on workshops that you feel drawn to.

- You could also join groups of like-minded people who inspire you.

- And you may end up wanting to share your inspiration and enthusiasm with others too.

  (Note – Gain Eco knowledge by looking at the 'Sustainable Living and Eco-Friendly' section near the back of the book, see page 123).

Chapter 18.
Keep an open mind.

'A person who never made a mistake
never tried anything new'.
(Albert Einstein).

18 – Keep an open mind.

- Be curious.

- Think all possibilities.

- Don't limit yourself, (and put yourself in a box).

- Be flexible.

- Get out of your comfort zone sometimes.
  Step into the unknown.

- Think, 'I can' rather than 'I can't'.

- Challenge yourself.
  Try something new and surprise yourself.

- Failure is only a stepping stone to success.

18 – Keep an open mind.
(Expanded chapter).

When you have an open mind it allows you to see the bigger picture.
And not get stuck in narrow-mindedness.

This can help you to be more flexible and to see things differently from a fresh perspective.

It can feel safe to stay with what we know, but sometimes it's good to get out of our comfort zone. It makes it easier to step into the unknown and to try new things without preconceptions.

When you stop limiting yourself, you may find that you can do all kinds of things that you didn't think you could!

Stepping into the unknown can seem scary, but when you let go of the fear of getting it all wrong, suddenly life can become exciting!

<u>18 – Keep an open mind.</u>
<u>(Practical exercises).</u>

- Is there anything that you have always wanted to do but felt afraid to try?

- What is holding you back? (Fear of the unknown? Fear of failure?)

- Try something new.
  Something you feel drawn to.
  (e.g. learning a new language, learning to play a musical instrument or simply joining a club of like-minded people).

- Get out of your comfort zone sometimes.
  You might surprise yourself and find that you can cope.
  You might even enjoy yourself!
  New possibilities may start to open up for you.

Chapter 19.
Have fun, play & laugh.

'In everyone there is a hidden child
wanting to play'.
(Friedrich Nietzsche).

19 – Have fun, play & laugh.

- Make time to relax and enjoy yourself.

- Do fun things with your family.

- Laugh with your friends.

- Be creative.

19 – Have fun, play & laugh.
(Expanded chapter).

Sometimes we can be so busy in life that we forget to spend some time relaxing and doing what we enjoy.

In our fast-paced world it is easy to work too hard and to overdo things . (This can even lead to burnout).

Doing fun activities, having a laugh and being creative can help you to unwind and to recharge your batteries.

'All work and no play makes Jack a dull boy' is an old English saying.

It's good to have a balance of work and play in our lives.

19 – Have fun, play & laugh.
(Practical exercises).

- Make sure that you schedule in some fun, play time in your life. Set some regular time aside just for that.

- Find ways to laugh!
  e.g. read funny books, watch funny films, tell jokes together, go and see a stand-up comedian.

  Laughing is good for you! It releases Endorphins, (sometimes called the happy hormone) which helps to relieve pain, reduce stress and improve your sense of well-being.
  It triggers positive feelings and helps you to relax, feel peaceful and happy.
  (Endorphins are also released by exercise and doing pleasurable activities).

- Be creative. (Even if you think you aren't!)
  Having a little creative project can help you to calm down, be expressive and get your mind off stressful thoughts.
  There are many different ways to be creative.
  e.g. art, writing, dancing to your favourite music or playing a musical instrument, cooking, gardening, decorating or making and building something etc.

Chapter 20.
Don't take yourself
too seriously.

'Don't take life too seriously.
You will never get out of it alive'.
(Elbert Hubbard).

20 – Don't take yourself too seriously.

- Be a bit detached.

- Be objective.

- Having a sense of humour helps you to see things in perspective.

20 – Don't take yourself too seriously.
(Expanded chapter).

It is easy to take ourselves far too seriously and to get lost in the stress and drama of life.

If we can stop and see ourselves from the outside, we can often make things a lot easier for ourselves.

Having a sense of humour can be a great help.
Seeing the funny side of life, even in difficult circumstances, can lighten the situation and help you and everyone feel much better.

<u>20 – Don't take yourself too seriously.</u>
<u>(Practical exercises).</u>

- If you are starting to feel stressed, try stopping for a while and observing yourself, (as if you were watching someone else).

   This can help you to see yourself from a distance and to notice the absurdity that happens to us all sometimes in life. It can help you to have compassion for yourself and maybe even to see the 'funny' side of what is happening.

- It can be fun sometimes to 'step out of yourself' and to pretend to be someone else for a while!

   If it doesn't sound too challenging, you could try transforming yourself into a different character by dressing up in clothes you don't normally wear.

   A trip to the local charity shop may lead to all kinds of interesting dressing up options.

   Simply trying on different hats can be a lot of fun and can help you to not take yourself too seriously.

Chapter 21

Simpify, clarify & de-clutter.

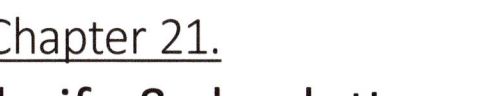

'The less baggage you carry
the lighter you will feel'.

21 – Simplify, clarify & de-clutter.

- Helps you to think more clearly and to feel free.

- Let go of the past, (anything that is holding you back).

- What is important in life?

- Make your environment beautiful.

- Simplify.
  Instead of thinking, 'What can I add'?
  think, 'What can I remove'?

21 – Simplify, clarify & de-clutter.
(Expanded chapter).

It is all too easy to accumulate all kinds of possessions and material goods.

Sometimes it can build up to be so cluttered that we can't find anything anymore!

We often hang on to things associated with the past. This can be good for happy memories but sometimes it is necessary to let go of the past, have a clear out and make space for the new.

Often just letting go and having more space can feel freeing.

Although having lots of material goods or buying the latest item can make us feel happy for a while, it is often fleeting.

What is important in life?

Sometimes the simply things like being with our family or going for a walk in Nature is all that we need to feel happy and connected.

21 – Simplify, clarify & de-clutter.
(Practical exercises).

- Sometimes we can get overwhelmed by so much stuff that it can be good to de-clutter.
  You could recycle some items, sell them or donate them to a charity shop or organisation.

- It can feel good to simplify.
  Try clearing your room.
  Deleting old emails (and unsubscribing if you are getting too many).
  Sorting and reducing the number of your digital photos.
  And spending less time on Social Media.

- It is easy to get overwhelmed and distracted by all the information in our world today.

- Try clarifying what it is that is most important for you.
  Focus on that.

  (Note – for ideas on recycling, look at the 'Sustainable Living and Eco-Friendly' section near the back of the book, see page 123).

Chapter 22.
Go with the flow.

'If life gives you lemons,
make lemonade'.
(Elbert Hubbard).

<u>22 – Go with the flow.</u>

- Everything happens for a reason.
  (But it might not be obvious why until later)!

- Dance with life.

- Don't try and be in control all the time.

- Let go and see where it leads you.
  (But don't be irresponsible).

- If you think you're right, you may be wrong.
  Don't be too rigid in your thinking.

22 – Go with the flow. (Expanded chapter).

We often want to remain in control of our lives all the time, reluctant to let go and to go with the flow.

Although it can be good to be organised and to have our intentions of things we want to do, there is also a time to let go.

If we try and force things it can lead to frustration if they don't work out the way we want them to.

So, as well as planning, allow things to happen.
It can lead to wonderful surprises!

Make room for spontaneity.

Notice synchronicity or 'happy accidents', (in truth there are no 'accidents').

22 – Go with the flow. (Practical exercises).

- We often complicate life by over-thinking.
  Think less and feel more.
  Come from the heart not the head.

- And tune into your 'gut' feelings.
  What is your intuition telling you?
  What feels 'right' or 'wrong' to you?
  (Not necessarily what everyone else is doing).
  Follow your inner voice.

- Sometimes opportunities or people appear in your
  life, unexpectedly, as if by accident.
  But there are no 'accidents'.
  What can you learn from these happenings?
  Where are you being led?

Chapter 23.
Enjoy where you are.

'This moment
you are in exactly the place you need to be'

<u>23 – Enjoy where you are.</u>

- Remember to <u>be </u>as well as to do.

- Enjoy being in the present moment.

- Life is simple. Don't make it too complicated.

- Be grateful with what you already have and for where you are right now.

- Sometimes the journey can be more fun than the destination.

23 – Enjoy where you are.
(Expanded chapter).

It is easy to spend time dwelling on the past or thinking about the future.

But in the process, we forget to be here in the present moment.

When we stop and remember to be alive in the here and now, we can start to notice everything around us. We begin to see things that previously we hadn't been aware of. (This is often called 'Mindfulness').

Even the smallest or simplest things can suddenly appear amazing and wonderful, like watching an insect fly by, hearing a beautiful bird song or looking at the incredible detail of a flowerhead.
(Even mundane objects in your house can suddenly take on a simple beauty of their own).

And in that all-consuming moment, we can forget about any worries and concerns we might have. It's as if they just fade away and we can be filled with a peaceful bliss instead.

23 – Enjoy where you are.
(Practical exercises).

.....a moment of peace in a busy, stressful world.....

- Stop and Listen.......what can you hear?
- Look around.......what can you see?

  Spend as long as you want doing this.
  Connect to the here and now.
  (And in doing so you can connect with the peace inside you).

- Remember.....

  The past has gone,
  the future is yet to come.
  This present moment, the here & now,
  is all we really have.
  Enjoy it!

Chapter 24.
Accept everyone!

'It's simpler to love everyone
rather than having to decide who'.

24 – Accept everyone!

- We're all equal.

- No-one is better than anyone else.

- Let go of judgement and criticism.

- Have compassion.

- Accept our differences, we're all unique.

- Accept everyone, whatever colour, nationality, religion, (or no religion), gender, sexual orientation, 'disability', class, education, size, shape, hair style, (or no hair...) or any other perceived 'weirdness'.

24 – Accept everyone!
(Expanded chapter).

It can be very easy to judge other people by their appearance, (colour, nationality, class or clothes they wear etc).

But that can be just their external image and not what is actually inside.

Ultimately we are all unique individuals and equal. It might not appear so because we tend to think in terms of education, wealth, health, status and 'success'.

But we are all human beings and we all share that in common.

When we realise this we can start to accept our differences and uniqueness and we can begin to enjoy each other and ourselves.

Despite our outside appearance, circumstance and opinions, we all want to be understood, respected and appreciated. We all want to be loved and feel like we belong.

24 – Accept everyone!
(Practical exercises).

- Do you have any preconceived ideas about certain people that might not actually be true?

- Don't compare yourself with others, (we are all different).

- When we interact with different people, we can start to better understand ourselves, (our own ideas, beliefs and values).

- Don't try to control others.
  Stop trying to change people to be more like the people you want them to be, but instead accept them as they are.
  Let them think and feel in their own way.

- Don't focus on the negative in someone else and what you don't like about them. Instead focus on the positive and what you do like about them. Focus on what you do have in common.

- Even when accepting everyone, you can still choose your friends.
  You can decide who you want to spend time with.

Chapter 25.
<u>Where are all the men?</u>

'Being loving & caring
isn't just for women'!

25 – Where are all the men?

- Self-help and spiritual groups are often mainly women.

- But being loving and caring isn't just for women!

- Because the 'old' belief system is that men should be hard and tough, it can be more difficult for them to find and show their 'softer' sides.

- We all have some masculine and feminine qualities no matter which gender we are.

25 – Where are all the men?
(Expanded chapter).

There has often been a general view that in order to be a 'real' man you have to be tough, hard, aggressive and competitive.
And you shouldn't show any 'weakness', vulnerability or 'soft' emotions. (This can be considered too 'feminine').

But those qualities aren't just for women.

So it can be harder for men to be emotional, get in touch with themselves, admit there is anything wrong, ask for help or get into self-help.

We all have some masculine and feminine qualities. 'Lower' aspects of these are aggression and dominion in men and stagnation and disempowerment in women. If we think of the 'higher' best qualities of us, (that are sometimes referred to as the Divine Feminine and the Divine Masculine) although they are both within all of us, here are some differences,

Women – nurturing, gentle, patient, reflective, pausing, holding, creating, birthing ideas, intuition, being.
Men – confidence, focus, courage, action, direction, protection, boundaries, standing up for what is right, acting on our intuition, doing.

A balance of these two helps to create a better world.

25 – Where are all the men?
(Practical exercises).

- If you are a man, do you find it hard to get in touch with your 'softer' sides? Nurturing, gentle, patient, intuitive?
  You might want to get more connected to this part of you.

- To do this you could try -
  Allowing yourself to feel more vulnerable sometimes. If possible find other people who you feel safe with. (This might be family or close friends or you may consider seeing a therapist?)
  You can also connect to yourself through writing in a journal.

- Don't be afraid to help and support others in a caring way. Or even to let yourself cry at movies!

- Whether you are man or a woman, it could be good to embrace all the qualities of the Divine Feminine and the Divine Masculine.

Chapter 26.
Serve others.

'Happiness is never decreased by being shared'.
(Buddha).

26 – Serve others.

- Help everyone.

- Work together.

- Co-operate, (a win-win situation).

- It's not just about you.

- Give something back to your community.

- Share your skills.

<u>26 – Serve others.</u> (Expanded chapter).

Although looking after yourself is very important, (and you can't give to others from an empty cup) it's not just about you!

There is a joy and satisfaction in helping others too.

There's a time for doing things yourself and a time for being with other people.

Sometimes it is good to have some quiet, 'me' time on your own, for rest and reflection and to recharge your batteries.

But too much of this can lead to you feeling lonely.

It's good to get a balance in life.

Often things feel better shared.

And when we work together and support each other, suddenly the world becomes a better place.

It becomes a win-win situation, (rather than just trying to beat everyone and be better than everyone else).

<u>26 – Serve others.</u> (Practical exercises).

- In what ways could you help others?

- What skills, talents and enthusiasms could you share?

- Try volunteering, (giving some of your time and skills for free, to help a good cause).

- You could start a club or group to help others or to share your enthusiasms.
  And you'd make some new like-minded friends too, (a win-win situation!)

- Try giving kindness for no apparent reason other than it feels good, (and it makes others feel good too).
  It spreads like a ripple around the world!

Chapter 27.
We're all in this together.

'When we see the night sky full of stars
we get a sense of our place in it all'.

<u>27 – We're all in this together.</u>

- We all share in common the experience of being human.

- We're all one!

- Treat others as you would like to be treated yourself.

- Think 'Unity' of everyone, (not separation).

27 – We're all in this together.
(Expanded chapter).

We are all going through big changes on planet Earth at this time, but we are going through it together.

We all know what it feels like to be human and so we can help and support each other through it all.

It's time to end the illusion of separation.
We are all connected, we are all one, there is unity of everyone.

27 – We're all in this together.
(Practical exercises).

- Try connecting with other people in a more friendly, accepting way.

- The more you connect, the less lonely and separate you will feel.

- Instead of just thinking, 'What can I get out of this for me'?, also think 'What can we all get out of this together'? 'What is the best for everyone'?

- Try connecting more deeply to everything – to yourself, others, Nature, planet Earth and a higher power, (sometimes called 'God' or the Universe – or see page 6 for other 'names').

   Ways to connect more might include, - journaling, (writing down your thoughts and feelings), accepting yourself and others without judgements, enjoying being out in Nature, sensing Mother Earth as an entity in her own right and embracing the idea of a higher, benevolent power.

Chapter 28.
We have a choice now.

'How wonderful it is that nobody need wait
a single minute before starting to improve the world'.
(Anne Frank).

28 – We have a choice now.

- We have the opportunity to change things for the better.

- To learn to love and heal ourselves, everyone and the planet Earth.

- Be the change you would like to see in the world.

- Look after the Earth and all the life forms we share it with. This is our beautiful 'home'.

28 – We have a choice now.
(Expanded chapter).

This is a time of great change on planet Earth.

It is affecting all of us, Nature and the Earth itself.

We have this opportunity now to change things for the better.

What would you like to see more of in our world in the future?

More peace, equality, unity, co-operation, acceptance, support, care & love?
For ourselves, for others, for Nature, (all the many different animals and plants) and for the planet Earth herself.

Don't wait for the world to change, you can start to change it right now.
It can start with you, whoever you are. Every little bit helps.

Together we can help to make a better, more beautiful world.

28 – We have a choice now.
(Practical exercises).

- What could you do today to help make the world a better place?

- You could find more peace and happiness in yourself, (e.g. by practising meditation and positive thinking). This automatically helps everyone because it spreads out and sends ripples around the world.

- You could volunteer or do some charity work.

- You could be more eco-friendly, (e.g. recycling and using green energy).

  Note – for more detail on sustainable living and eco-friendly tips & practices, see back of the book, (page 123).

Chapter 29.
What is real?

'Perception changes as we do'.

29 – What is 'real'?

- See beyond the illusions of life.

- You will start to wake up to what is really going on.

- Be open-minded.

- You are on a mission, but you have probably forgotten what it is. (Clue: What do you feel most passionate about?)

<u>29 – What is 'real'?</u> (Expanded chapter).

It is very easy to get caught up in the illusions or 'drama' of life.

We are often bombarded with distractions and information and are often told what to believe, what we should do and what is 'real'.

But actually there is a lot more going on under the surface than we realise.

The more you look for this, by keeping an open mind, the more 'truth' you will discover.

And by working to improve yourself and to help make the world a better, more peaceful place, you will start to wake up to what is really going on.

You will start to find your special, unique mission, (or life purpose) and you will begin to find true happiness for yourself and for everyone.

<u>29 – What is real?</u> (Practical exercises).

- What is your 'calling? (However 'big' or 'small'). What do you love to do? What do you feel most passionate about? What do you feel in your heart?

- Although there are a lot of 'negative' things happening in the world, there are also a lot of 'positive' ones too.
  Everywhere more 'positive' things are starting to happen.

- Search them out.
  Focus on them.

- This is not hiding our heads in the sand, but focusing on 'positive' solutions which will help bring them into 'reality'.

Chapter 30.
Why wait?

'Don't leave it till it's too late –
live your life now'.

<u>30 – Why wait?</u>

- Do it now!

- Before it's too late.

- Life is short, (have no regrets).

- 'I thought that growing old would take a much longer time'.

30 – Why wait? (Expanded chapter).

Life goes by fast!

When you are young it seems like a long time, but when you get older you realise how quickly it went past!

So if possible, don't wait too long to do what you really want to do.

Do it now, before it's too late.

And in the current world situation, there is no time to lose.

This is the moment now, to start to change things for the better, for yourself, for everyone and for the planet Earth too.

30 – Why wait? (Practical exercises).

- If you knew you were going to die soon, what would you do now?

- Maybe there are some things you've never done but that you've always wanted to?
  You might not be able to do them all, but if you managed to do even some of those things, you might feel less regret. (But don't beat yourself up about it, remember to enjoy yourself where you are now).

- Focus on what you love to do the most.

- This could be 'big' things or 'small' things.
  It could be travelling to other countries or simply giving more time and love to family and friends.

- Often it is about having the courage to be our 'real' selves.
  And not just living a life that others want, but living the life that we want. And finding ways to be that.

- Don't wait!
  In whatever way you want to help and improve yourself, everyone and the world, start now!

  This is the time!

- Be Yourself.
- Come from Love.
- For the Highest Good of All.

Conclusion.

This book is a beginner's guide, to point you in the right direction.

There is a lot more for you to discover if you want to look further. (For a list of 'teachers' who have inspired me, see 'Acknowledgements' and there are many more people to find.)

Whatever 'speaks' to you and whatever you feel drawn to. They are all saying the same thing, but in different ways, from different perspectives. To appeal to different people.

As well as learning from others, ultimately you have all the answers for your best, unique self within you.

So I want to encourage you to find your own answers too by listening to your own feelings, intuition, (inner teacher) or 'Higher Self', (your direct connection to a Higher Source or 'God').

You are a unique, individual Human Being. You do count, whoever you are, wherever you are.

We are all an important piece of the jigsaw, contributing to the wholeness of life. (Universe is the unity of diversity).

We are learning to work together to love and heal ourselves, each other and the planet Earth.

The main message to remember is……

Move from fear to LOVE.

Focus on love, think love, be love.

Blessings!
Gavin Muschamp.

A final thought.....

We are each a unique, different jigsaw piece,
part of the bigger picture. Without you
the whole is not complete.
So it's important for you to be you!

And together we make up the whole picture.
Everyone has their part to play.
Working together towards a better, wonderful world.

Sustainable Living and Eco-Friendly tips & practices.

1 – Reduce, Re-use, Recycle.

*   Cut down on what you throw away, conserve natural resources and put less into landfill.
    (e.g. recycle paper and cans).
*   When shopping, take re-useable bags.
*   Buy products that are made of recycled materials.
*   Upcycle. A creative way to make old items into something new.
*   Instead of throwing things away, give them to local charity shops and organisations.

FACT: An estimated one-third of all food produced in the world is lost or wasted.

*   Eat up leftovers and use any spare ingredients to make interesting meals.
*   Give composting a try. Put less into landfill plus compost makes a great natural fertilizer.
*   Conserve Water. The less water you use, the less wastewater eventually ends up in the ocean.

2 – Choose Sustainable.

* Living a less consumerist lifestyle can benefit you and the planet. Buying less will save you money, reduce waste and improve your environmental footprint.

* Eat Sustainable Food.
  Buy organic - which is kinder on wildlife and better for you, (less additives) / Buy local, (cut down on air miles and support the local economy) / Eat less processed foods. / Grow your own fruit & veg.

FACTS: large scale food production accounts for about 25% of greenhouse emissions / Food production is a major cause of wildlife extinction. / One of the biggest causes of forest loss is using land to produce animal feed, (soy). / Producing meat creates vastly more carbon dioxide, (greenhouse emissions).

* Use Sustainable Energy, e.g. solar, wind and water power / support green energy companies.

* Choose non-toxic chemicals. Better for you and it doesn't send toxic chemicals into our waterways, (so better for wildlife too).

3 – Reduce Plastic Pollution.

* Avoiding plastic can divert a huge amount of waste from the oceans and landfill.
* Presently only about 9% of plastic gets recycled.

FACT: Around the world approximately 1 million plastic bottles are bought every minute.

4 – Live Energy Wise.

* Make your home more energy efficient, (and save money).
* Switch to LED's, (much longer lasting.)
* have proper house insulation.
* have efficient windows,

FACT: (25-30% of heat gain & loss is through the windows).

* consider a programmable thermostat, (to avoid running and wasting energy when you're not home).

5 – Walk, Bike or Take Public Transport.

* Drive less, reduce greenhouse gases and get some good exercise.
* Combine car trips, (e.g. school run and shopping).
* Carpool, share a car.

6 – Volunteer, Educate and Donate.

* Local nature reserves and parks are often looking for regular volunteers.
* Volunteer for clean-ups in your community.
* Support eco-friendly products. This encourages companies to source and produce their products in a sustainable way.
* Donate to environmental charities.
* Bank & invest ethically.

7 – Attract Wildlife to Your Garden.

* Grow pollinator friendly flowers to attract bees and butterflies.
* Have a pond.
* Put out food regularly for the birds in the winter.

8 – Plant a Tree.

* Trees provide food and oxygen. They help save energy, clean the air and help combat climate change. They are also a habitat for wildlife and they look beautiful!

Acknowledgements.

Here are some of the diverse people I've been inspired by and there are many more to find! (In alphabetical order).

Amma (Mata Amritanandamayi)
Sir David Attenborough
Richard Bach
Melanie Beckler
Rhonda Byrne
Eileen Caddy
Diana Cooper
Patricia Cota-Robles
Ram Dass
Mike Dooley
Dr Wayne Dyer
Jeff Foster
Thich Nhat Hanh
Louise Hay
Susan Jeffers
Mia Kafkios
Beth Kempton
Vex King
Leon Logothetis
Robin Sharma
Aletheia Luna and Mateo Sol
Anita Moorjani
Haemin Sunim
Greta Thunberg
Eckhart Tolle
Bronnie Ware
Tim Whild
Stuart Wilde
Oprah Winfrey
Maharishi Mahesh Yogi

Other acknowledgements & locations of photos.

* T-shirts from 'Chargrilled' on p23 / p35 / p83 / p103 / 131.
* p23. Location - Market Place, Wirksworth, Derbyshire, England.
* p31. Location - South Bank, London.
* p35. Location - Greenhill, Wirksworth, Derbyshire, England.
* p47 & p55. Location - Findhorn Foundation Community, Moray, Scotland.
* p63. Location - Cromford, Derbyshire, England.
* p71. With 'Brightlight' (my unicorn) and 'Leyline' (my dragon).
* p79. Location - Wirksworth recycling area.
* p83. Location - Matlock Bath, Derbyshire, England.
* p95. Location - Chalice Well Gardens, Glastonbury, Somerset, England.
* p99. NHS - National Health Service, England. (During Covid).
* p103. Location - St. Mary's Church, Wirksworth, Derbyshire, England.
* p107. Location - Matlock Youth4Climate Strike, Matlock, Derbyshire, England.
* p111. Reflection of me in my window.

Disclaimer.

I'm afraid there are no guarantees following the guidelines in this book, (although I sincerely hope they will hope).

It is not intended as a substitute for seeing a doctor or mental health expert. If you are having problems, (especially mental ones), it is recommended that you seek the relevant medical advice.

Appendix (i).

Appendix (ii).

Note-

The Appendix has been removed.

About the author.

Gavin Muschamp is interested in self-help, self-empowerment, spirituality and green issues.

A big catalyst for change occurred during a period of severe mental health problems.

He has been practising meditation for many years and has read widely on self-help and spiritual subjects. He spent 6 years living in spiritual communities.

He also has a BA Visual Arts and is an artist and writer who likes dressing-up, (but up until this point hadn't found an outlet for this secret passion!)

He lives in Wirksworth, a small quirky, characterful town on the edge of the Peak District National Park in Derbyshire, England. It is home to many artists and creative people. (There is an Arts Festival every year in September).

Special Award.

I am very honoured to have received this special award.

The 'Bath-tub' Award, 2023.
(Similar to a 'Bafta').

Writer
of the Year.
'Bath-tub Award.'
2023
Winners
Ceremony.
7-30pm

Writer
of the Year.

'Bath-tub Award.'

2023

Hurry up!

It starts
in 10 mins..

www.ingramcontent.com/pod-product-compliance
Lightning Source LLC
Chambersburg PA
CBHW040845120626

46547CB00001B/29

* 9 7 8 1 9 6 3 0 5 0 8 4 4 *